Sean Kenney

Cool
Creations

in

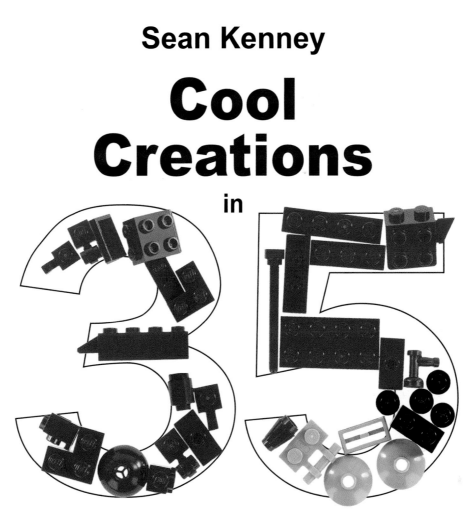

Pieces

Christy Ottaviano Books

Henry Holt and Company
New York

CONTENTS

The coolest thing about playing with my LEGO pieces is that I can build a million creations over and over with the same parts.

I wanted to see how many different creations I could make with the same 35 pieces. I started making a lot of the things you might expect: cars, robots, houses. But then I let my imagination go crazy. I built goofy faces and imaginary creatures to make my friends laugh, and I even built boring things like a stool and a vacuum. (Agh! Don't vacuum your LEGO pieces with your LEGO vacuum!)

So see if you can make some of the creations in this book. I've included lots of building instructions to get you started, but I bet that you can make even crazier contraptions than I did! When you're finished, put them online on www.mocpages.com/35 so I can see what you've made with just 35 pieces.

Have fun!

SEAN KENNEY

Here are the 35 pieces I've used throughout the book
for each creation and in various color schemes.

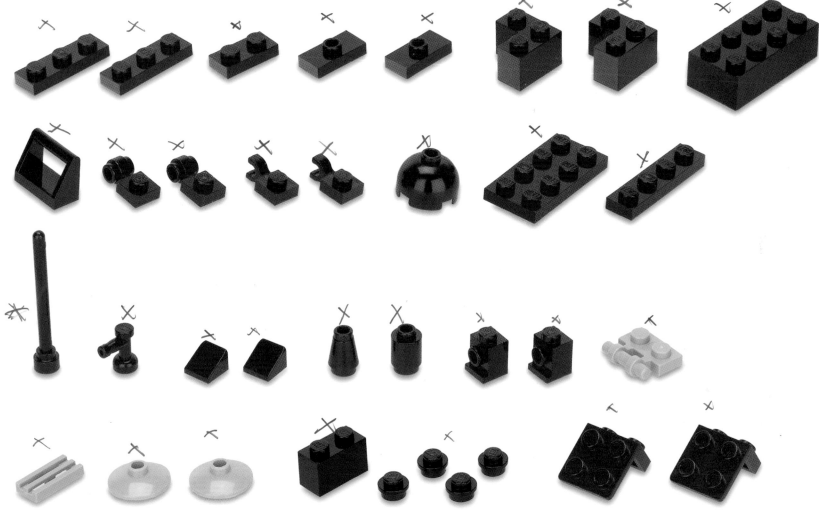

Need a few pieces? Visit seankenney.com/shop.

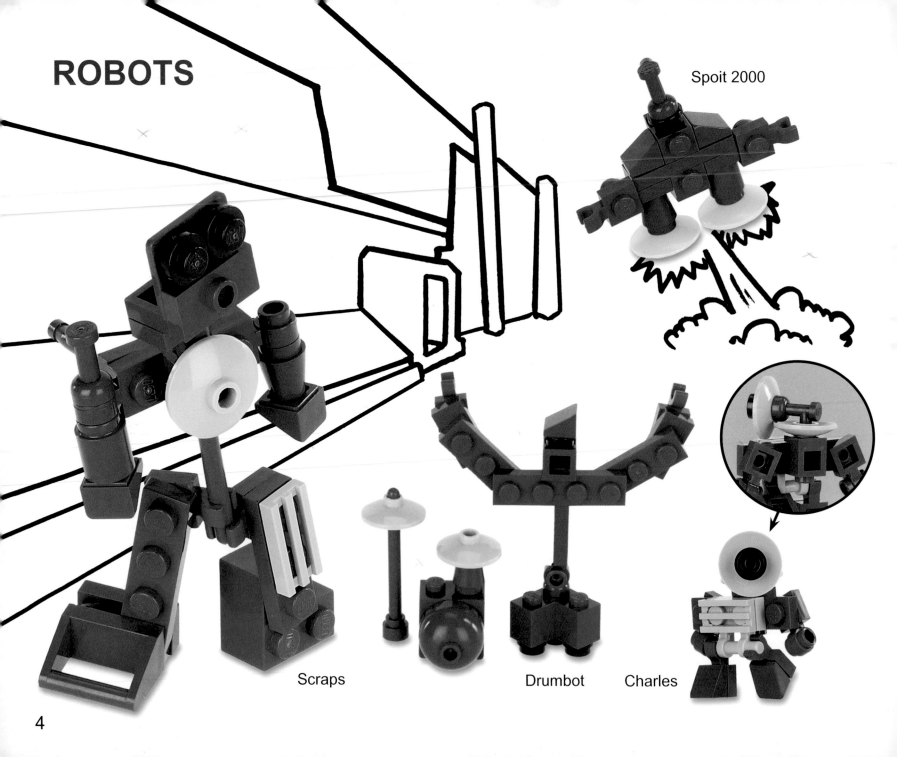

ROBOTS

Spoit 2000

Scraps

Drumbot

Charles

4

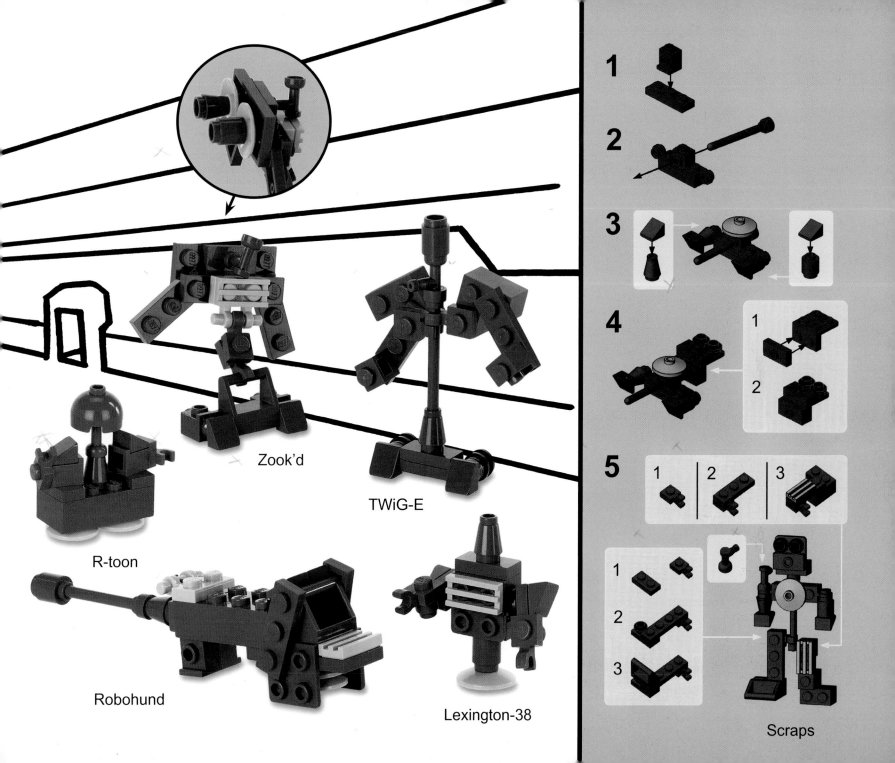

Zook'd

TWiG-E

R-toon

Robohund

Lexington-38

1

2

3

4

1

2

5

1 | 2 | 3

1

2

3

Scraps

MORE ROBOTS

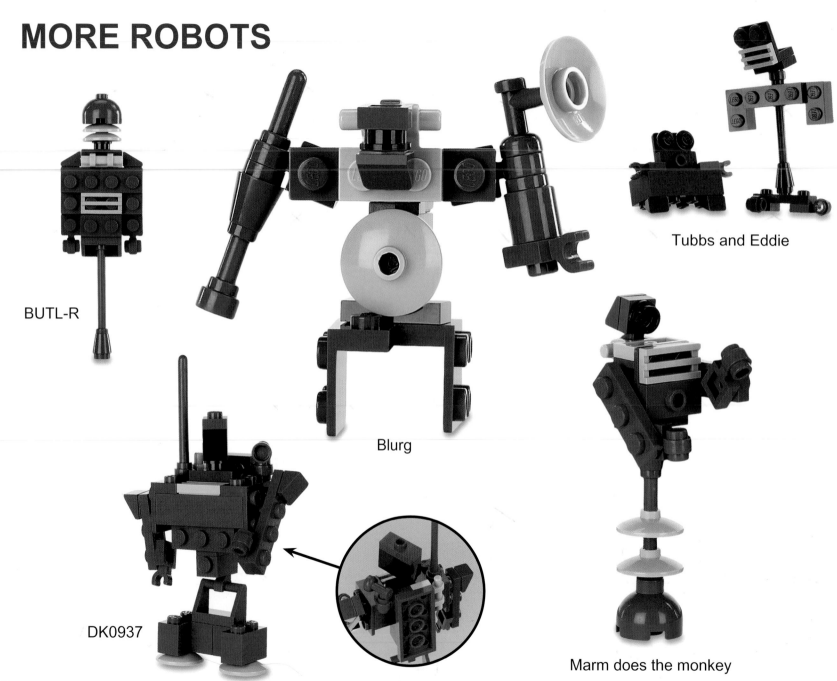

BUTL-R

Blurg

Tubbs and Eddie

DK0937

Marm does the monkey

6

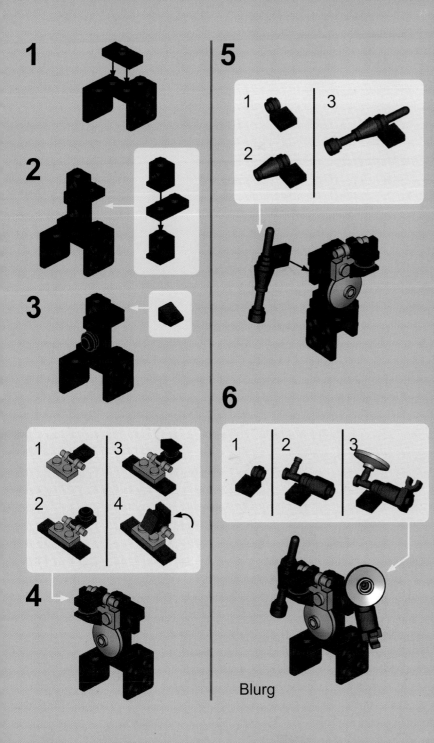

1

2

3

4

5

1
2
3

6

1 | 2 | 3

Blurg

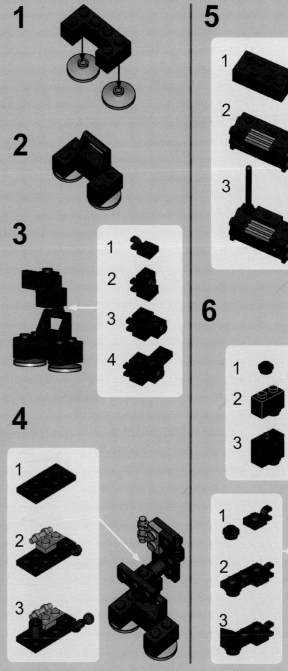

1

2

3

1
2
3
4

4

1
2
3

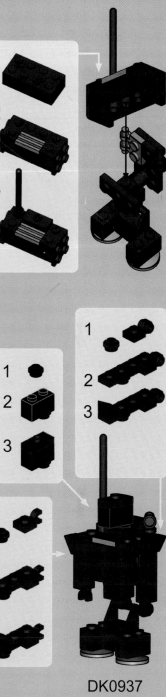

5

1
2
3

6

1
2
3

1
2
3

1
2
3

DK0937

TRANSFORMING ROBOTS

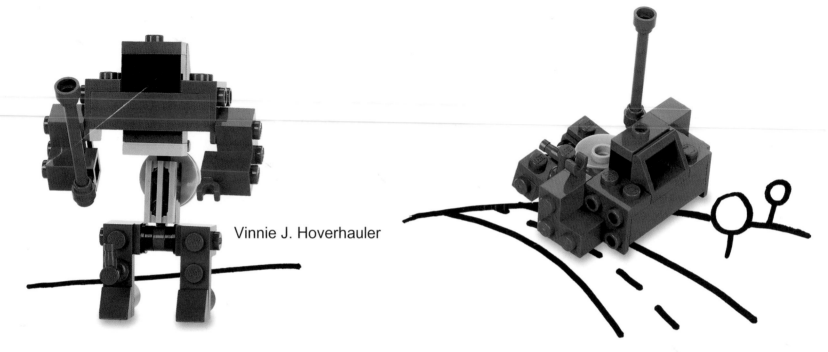

Vinnie J. Hoverhauler

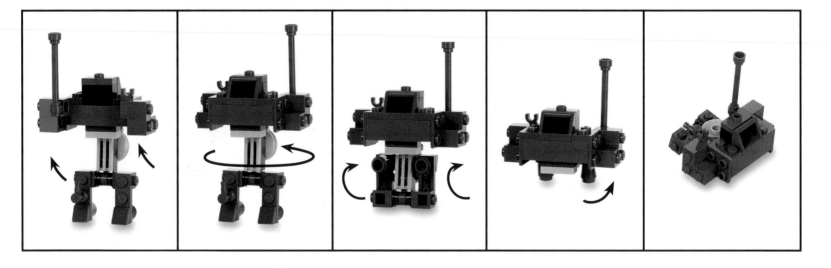

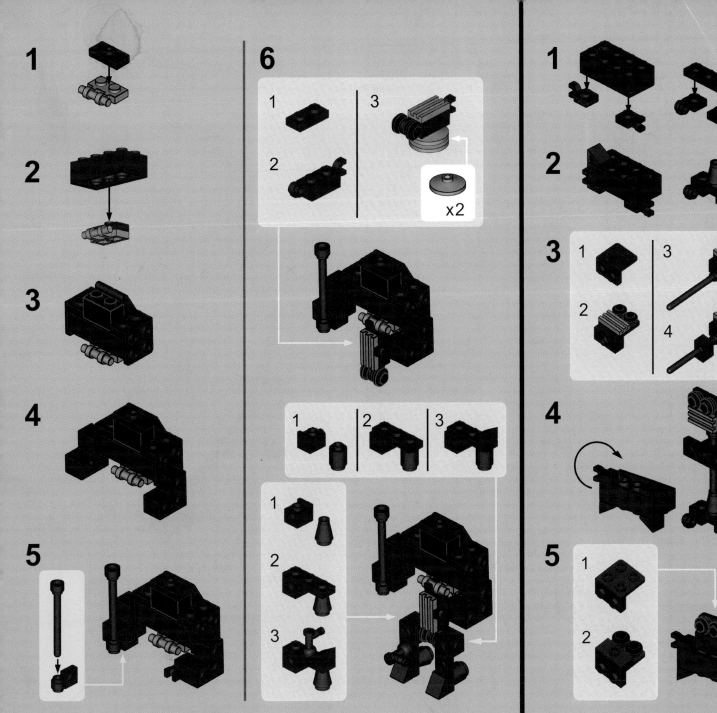

1

2

3

4

5

6

1

2

3

x2

1

2

3

1

2

3

Vinnie J. Hoverhauler

1

2

3

1

2

3

4

4

5

1

2

Tubbs and Eddie

SCI-FI SPACECRAFT

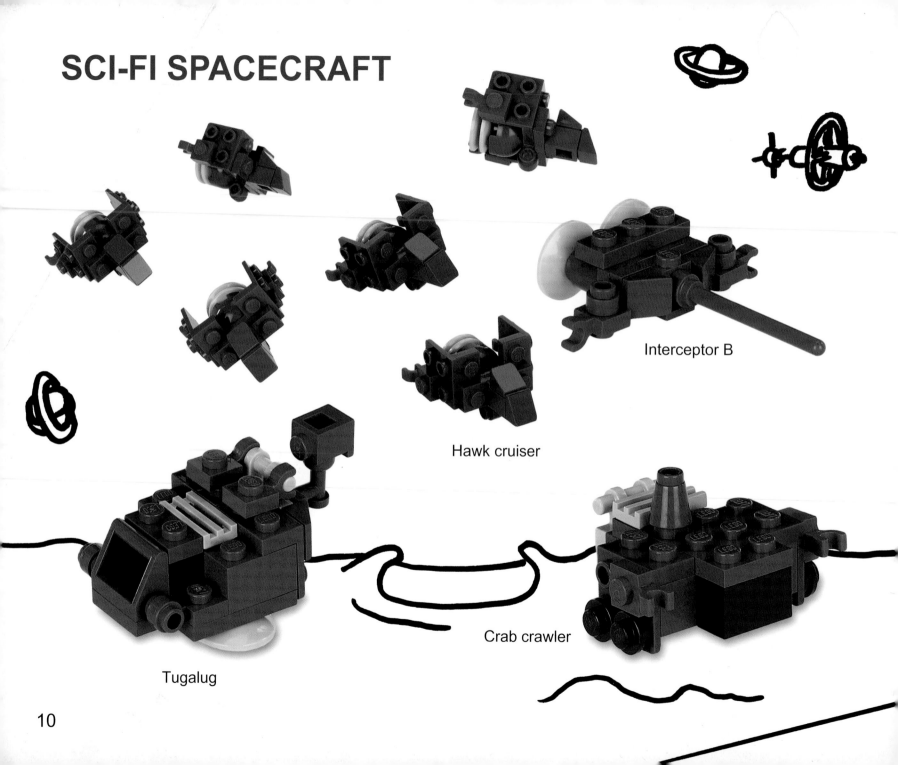

Interceptor B

Hawk cruiser

Tugalug

Crab crawler

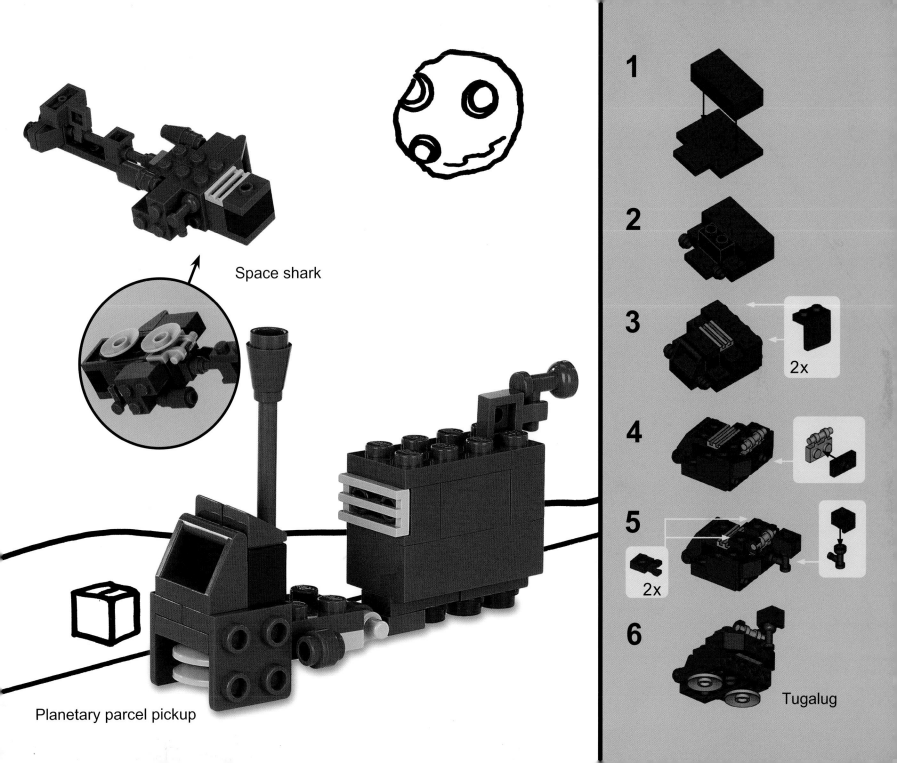

Space shark

Planetary parcel pickup

1

2

3 2x

4

5 2x

6 Tugalug

BUILDINGS

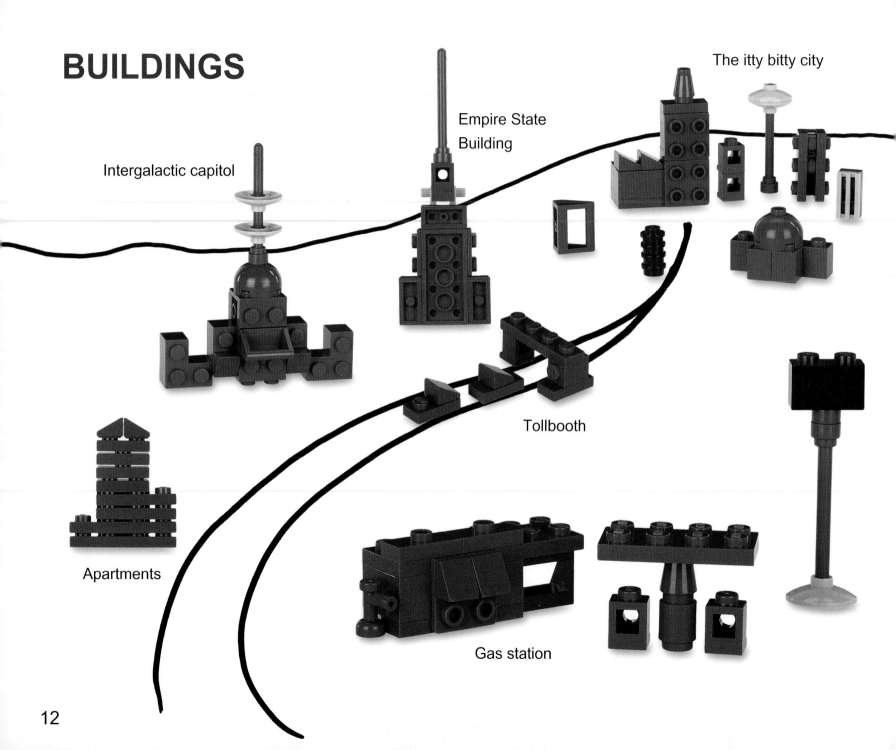

The itty bitty city

Empire State Building

Intergalactic capitol

Tollbooth

Apartments

Gas station

FURNITURE

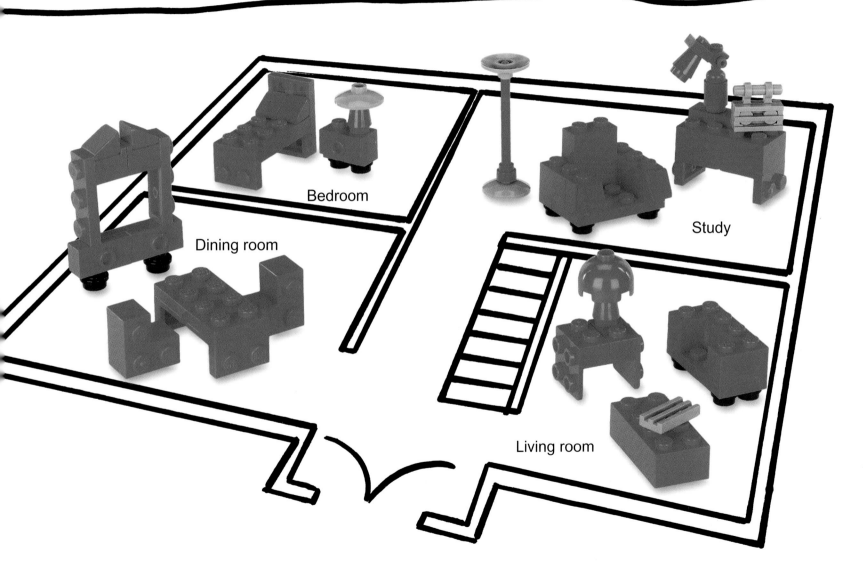

Bedroom

Dining room

Study

Living room

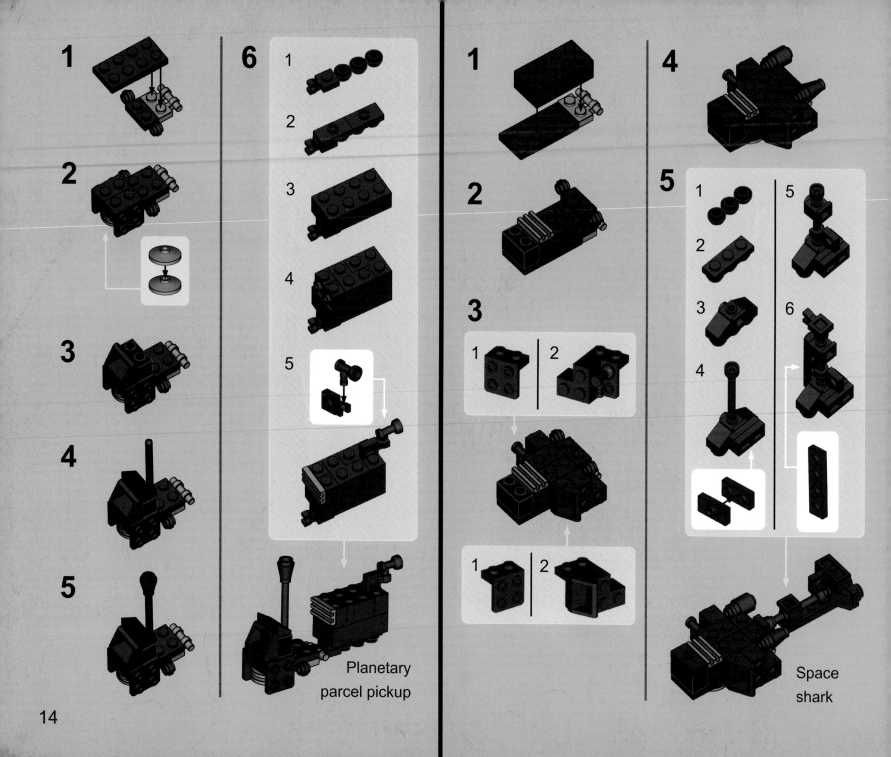

1

2

3

4

5

6
1
2
3
4
5

Planetary parcel pickup

1

2

3
1 | 2

1 | 2

4

5
1
2
3
4
5
6

Space shark

14

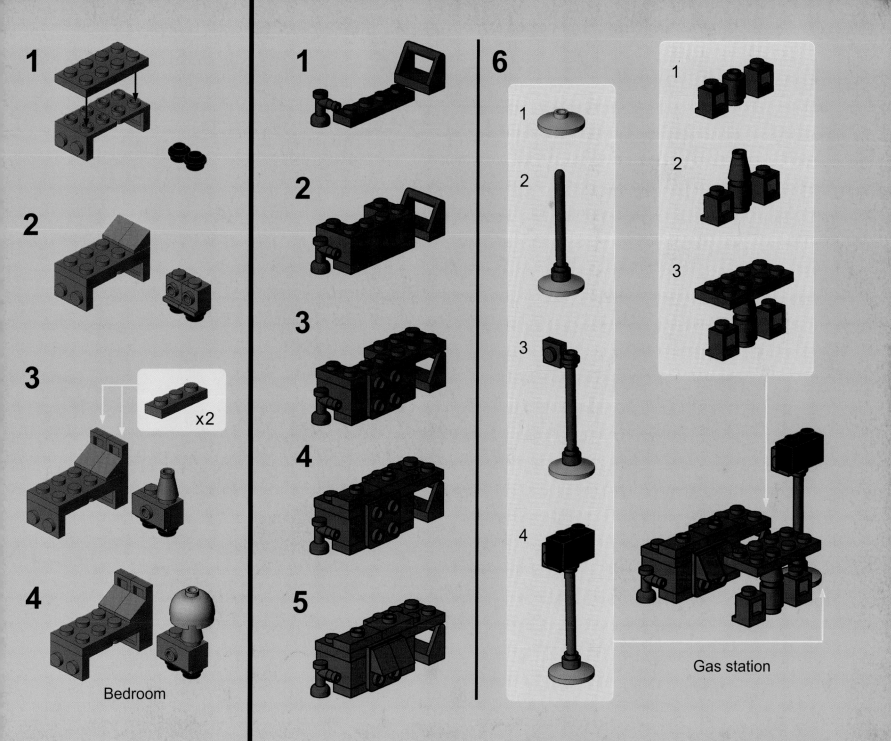

1

2

3

x2

4

Bedroom

1

2

3

4

5

6

1

2

3

4

1

2

3

Gas station

HOUSEHOLD OBJECTS

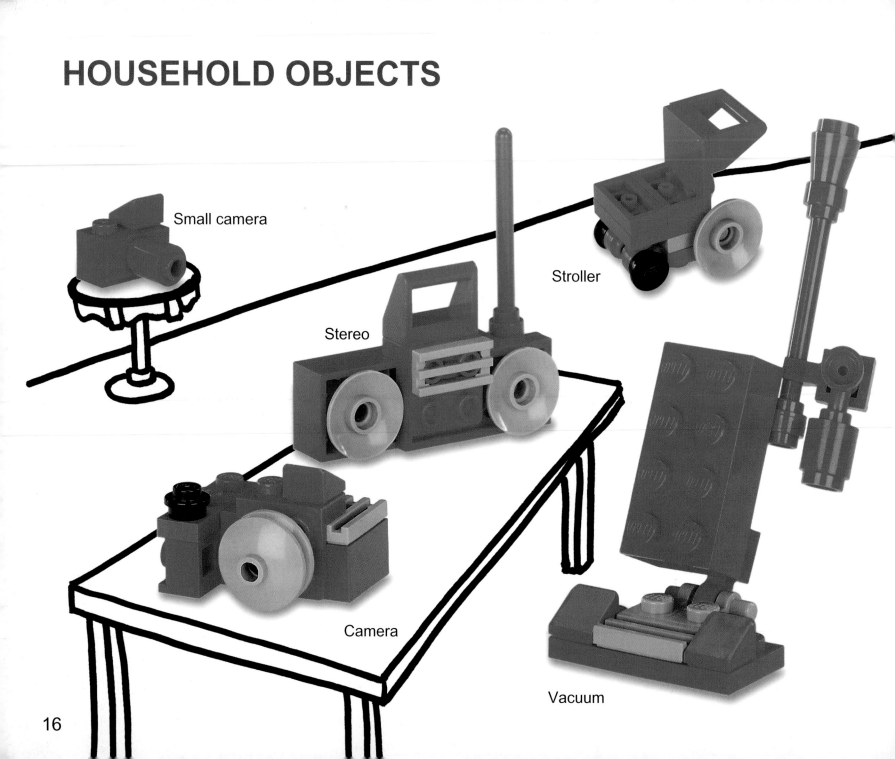

Small camera

Stroller

Stereo

Camera

Vacuum

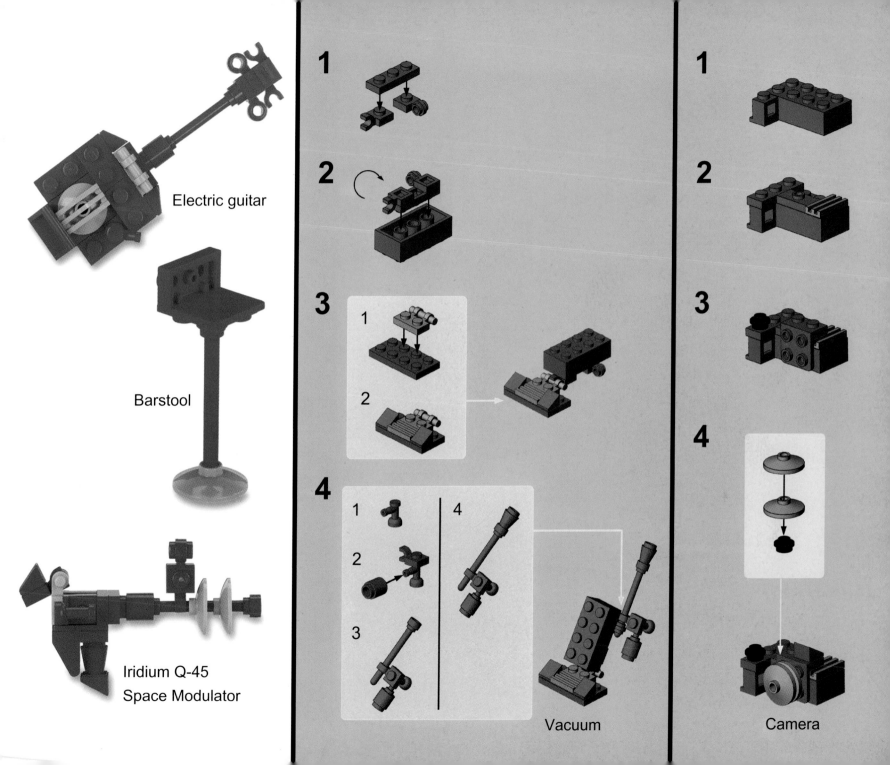

Electric guitar

Barstool

Iridium Q-45
Space Modulator

1

2

3
1
2

4
1
2
3
4

Vacuum

1

2

3

4

Camera

VEHICLES

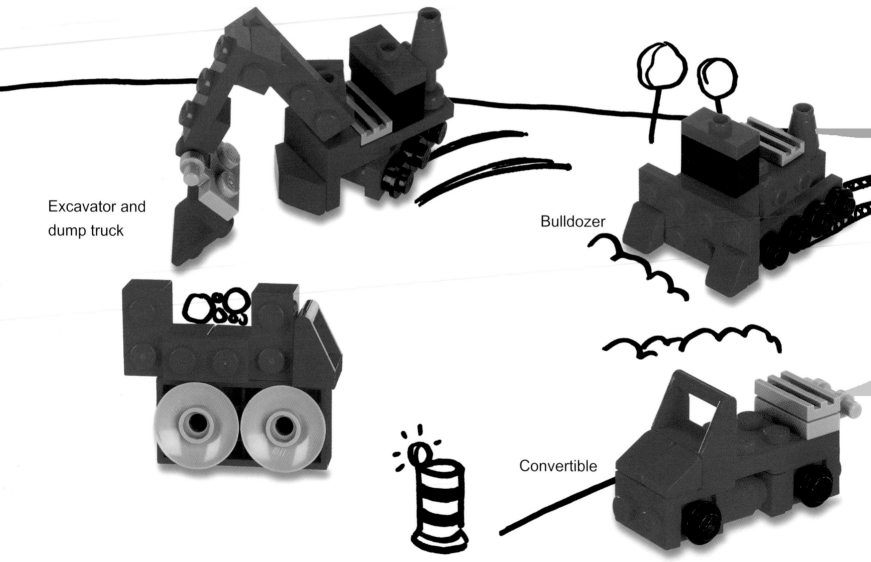

Excavator and
dump truck

Bulldozer

Convertible

Steam engine

Jumbo jet

Tow truck

Funny car

Minivan

Farm tractor

19

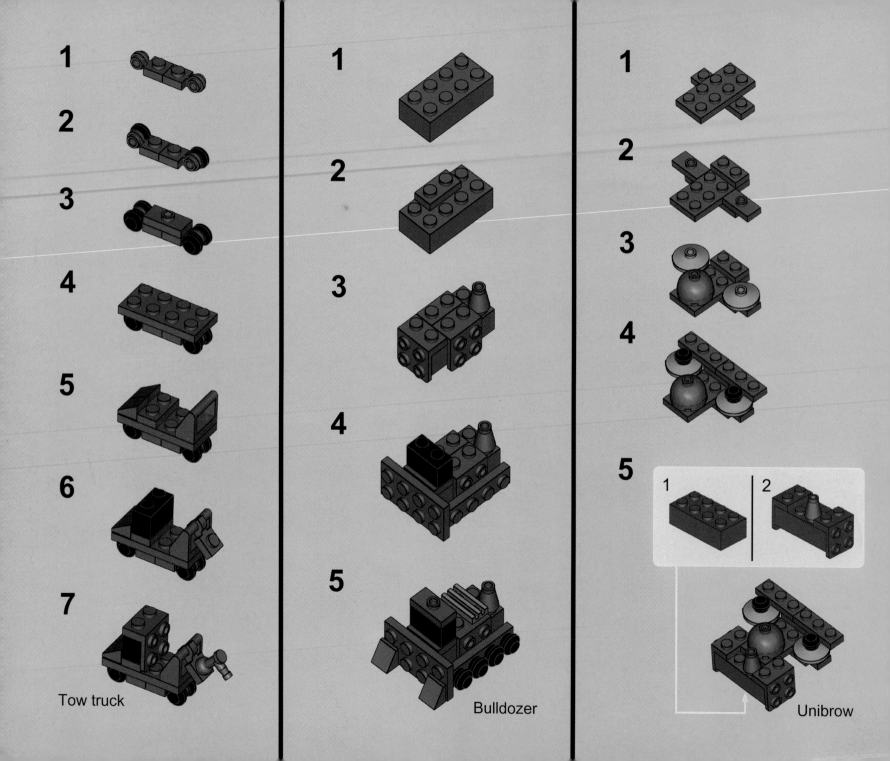

1

2

3

4

5

6

7

Tow truck

1

2

3

4

5

Bulldozer

1

2

3

4

5

1 | 2

Unibrow

GOOFY FACES

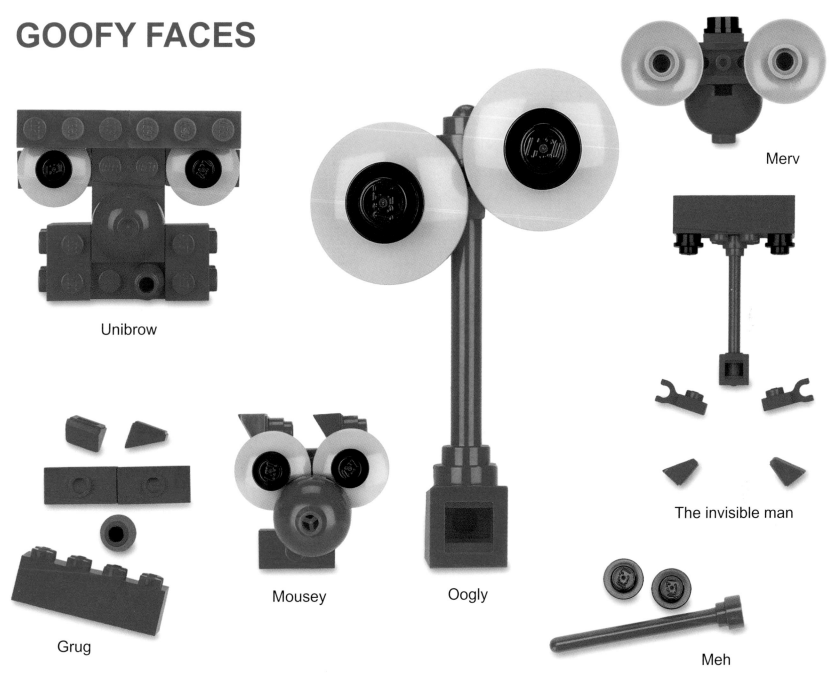

Unibrow

Merv

The invisible man

Grug

Mousey

Oogly

Meh

FROM THE RAINFOREST

Bat

Bullfrog

Gorilla

Manatee

22

Frog

Gecko

1

2

3

4

5

6
1
2
3

7
1
2
3

8
1
2
3
4

Gorilla

DOWN ON THE FARM

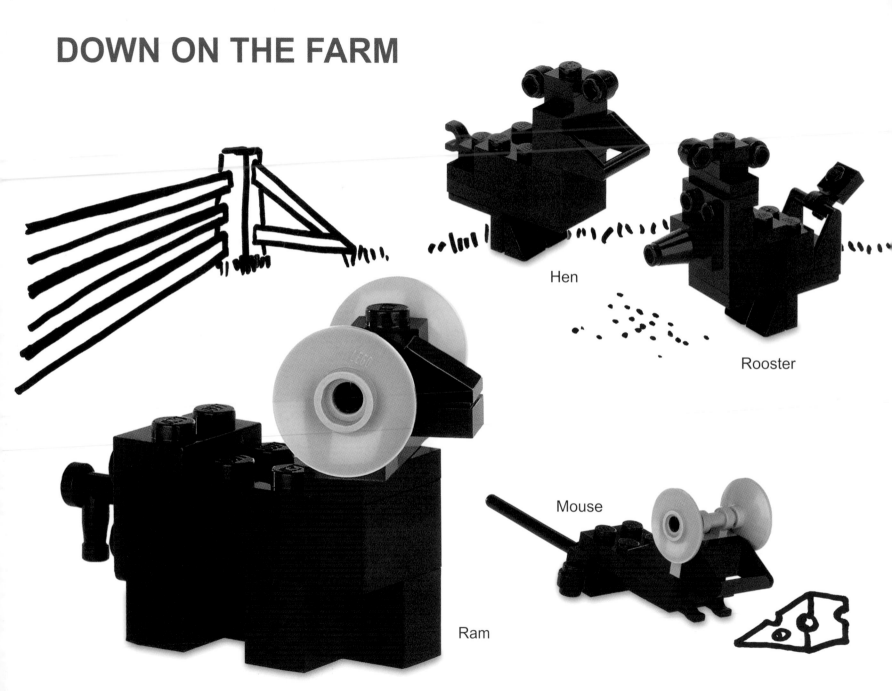

Hen

Rooster

Ram

Mouse

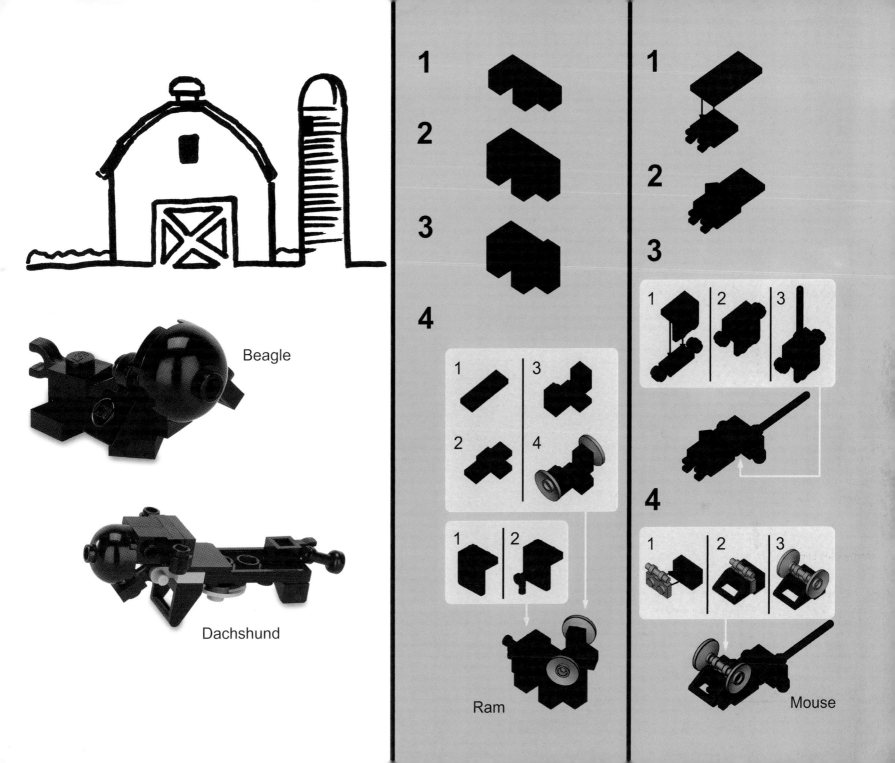

Beagle

Dachshund

1

2

3

4

1 | 3

2 | 4

1 | 2

Ram

1

2

3

1 | 2 | 3

4

1 | 2 | 3

Mouse

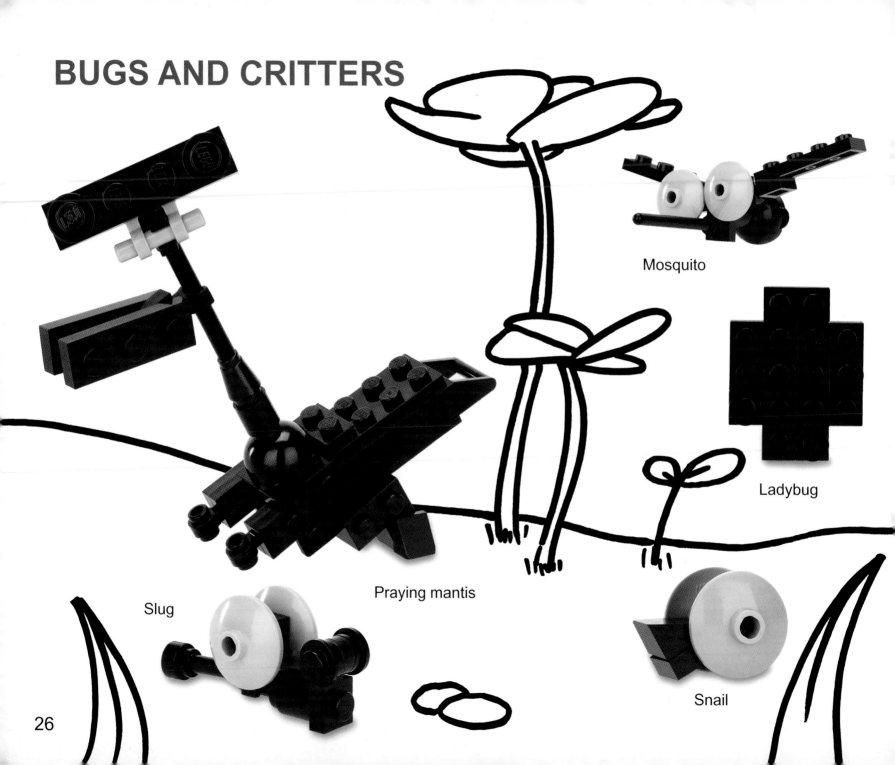

BUGS AND CRITTERS

Mosquito

Ladybug

Praying mantis

Slug

Snail

26

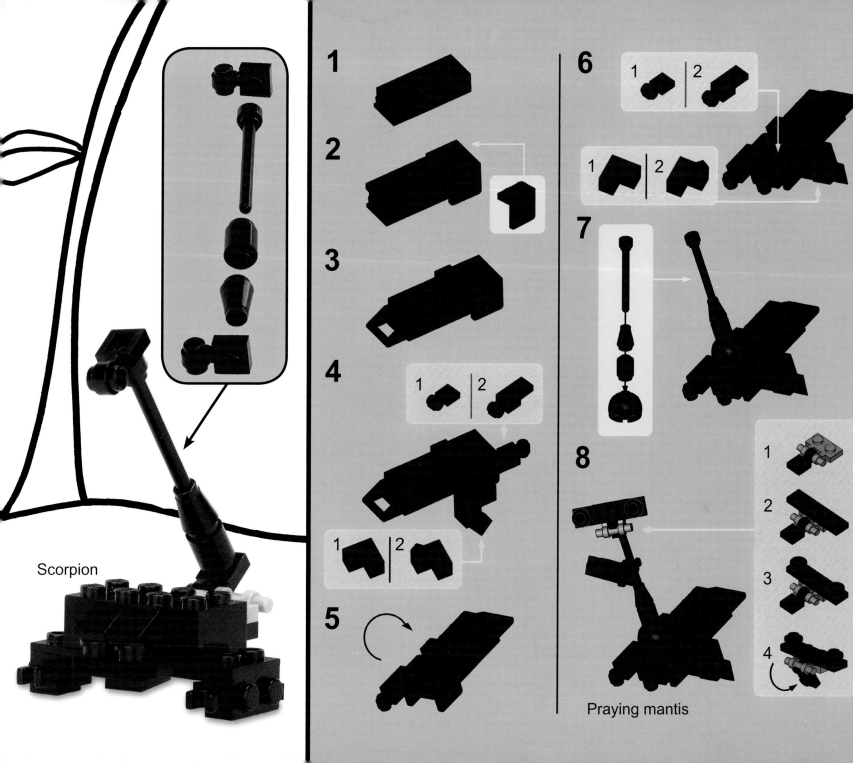

Scorpion

1

2

3

4

1 | 2

1 | 2

5

6

1 | 2

1 | 2

7

8

1

2

3

4

Praying mantis

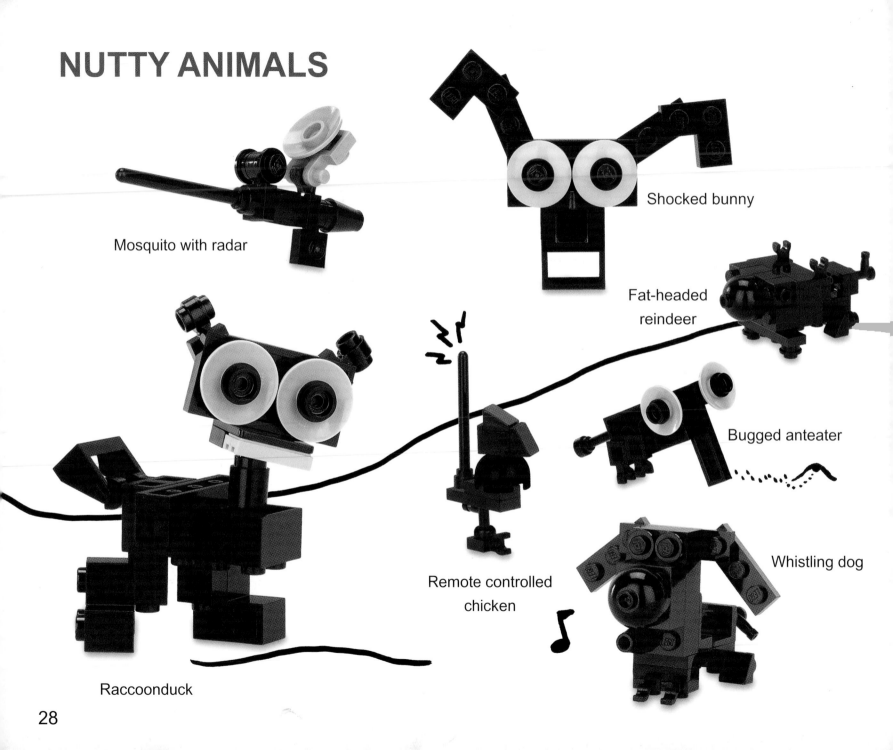

NUTTY ANIMALS

Mosquito with radar

Shocked bunny

Fat-headed reindeer

Bugged anteater

Raccoonduck

Remote controlled chicken

Whistling dog

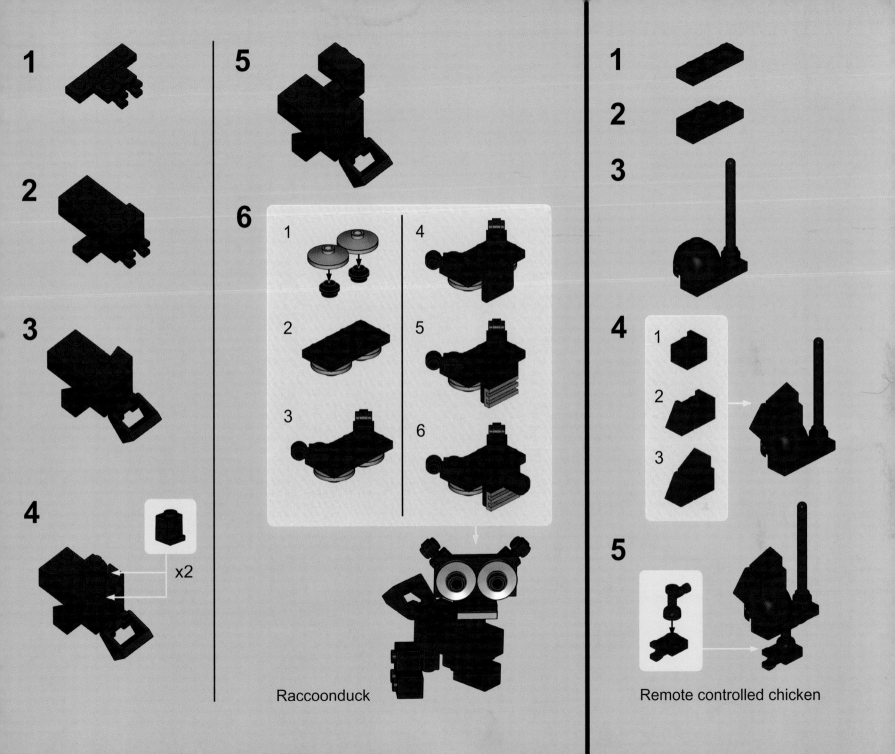

1

2

3

4 x2

5

6
1 2 3 4 5 6

Raccoonduck

1

2

3

4
1 2 3

5

Remote controlled chicken

ALIENS

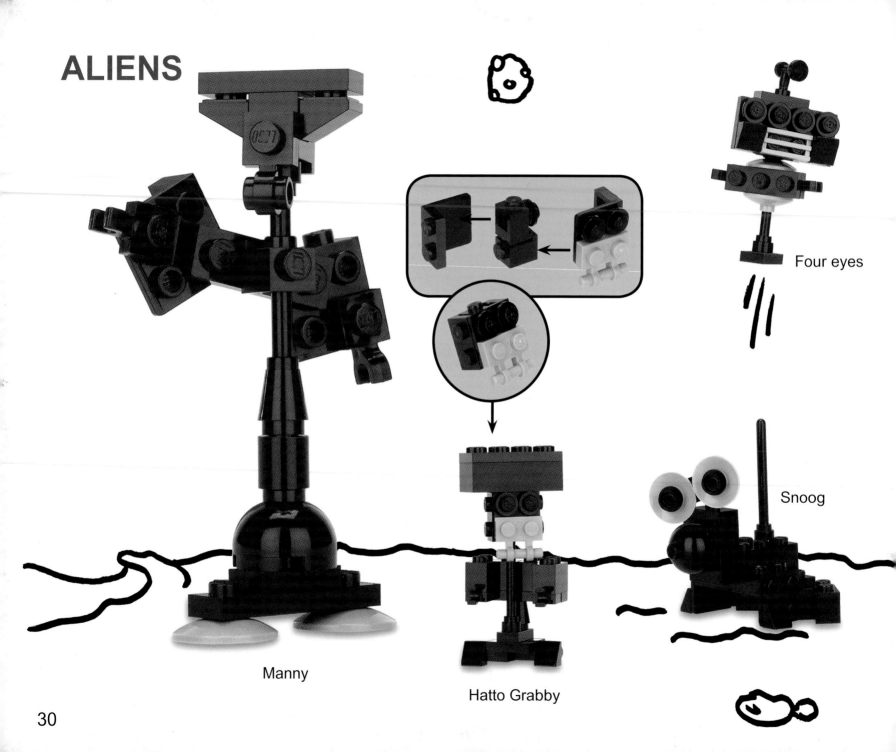

Four eyes

Snoog

Manny

Hatto Grabby

d-Spek

Buggley

Kevin

1

2

3

4 x2

5 | 1 | 2 | 3 |

1 x2 | 2

Snoog

For Tim

Henry Holt and Company, LLC
Publishers since 1866
175 Fifth Avenue
New York, New York 10010
mackids.com

Henry Holt® is a registered trademark of Henry Holt and Company, LLC.
Copyright © 2013 by Sean Kenney
All rights reserved.

LEGO®, the brick configuration, and the minifigure are trademarks of The
LEGO Group, which does not sponsor, authorize, or endorse this book.

Library of Congress Control Number: 2013935799
ISBN 978-0-8050-9692-7

Christy Ottaviano Books / Henry Holt Books for Young Readers may be
purchased for business or promotional use. For information on bulk purchases,
please contact Macmillan Corporate and Premium Sales Department at
(800) 221-7945 x5442.

First Edition—2013 / Book design by Elynn Cohen
LEGO bricks were used to create the models for this book.
The models were photographed by John E. Barrett.
Printed in China by Macmillan Production Asia Ltd.,
Kowloon Bay, Hong Kong (vendor code:10)

10 9 8 7 6 5 4 3 2 1

About Sean

Sean Kenney makes sculptures and models
out of LEGO bricks at his studio in New
York City and is recognized as one of the
premier LEGO brick builders in the world.
Visit Sean at seankenney.com.